Praye[illegible]
of the Fl[illegible]ove
of the Immacul[illegible]e Heart of Mary

PUBLISHED BY:

THE FLAME OF LOVE
OF THE IMMACULATE HEART OF MARY INC.
Postal Station Jacques-Cartier, PO Box 21111
Longueuil (Quebec) Canada J4J 5J4
Phone (579) -721-4027
www.theflameoflove.org
holymary@theflameoflove.org

ISBN: 978-1-989067-16-1

Second Edition

September 8, 2023
Nativity of the Virgin Mary

INTRODUCTION

This booklet contains all the prayers in use in the Cenacles of Prayer of the Flame of Love. These Cenacles can be done online or in our home with two or more people.

We encourage people to pray together the Flame of Love prayers to fulfill the request of our Lord Jesus and the Virgin Mary which are found in Elizabeth Kindelmann's Spiritual Diary.

Blinding Satan is the main goal, and it can be done in different ways which are described in the Diary.

Praying together is very important, it brings us together even if a long distance separates us. When we pray together, we are all united with Jesus.

It is not good to be alone, we have to learn from others and then we all walk with Jesus.

When we are together, Jesus is there and He looks at us because **"Where two or three have gathered together in My name, I am there in their midst"**. Mt 18, 20

These words are very important and we must take them to heart. Jesus encourages us to be many in prayer.

There is a time to be alone in our heart with Jesus and there is a time to be together, all in love with Jesus. Both are vital for our Christian life.

The cenacle leader decides who will read the message, say the prayers, meditate on the Rosary, and so on.

DETAILED TABLE OF CONTENT

"As we begin, use holy water and make the sign of the Cross: In the name of the Father, and of the Son and of the Holy Spirit. Amen."

PRAYER TO THE HOLY SPIRIT

Come Holy Spirit and fill the hearts of your faithful, enkindle in us the fire of Your love. Send forth Your Spirit and we shall be created, and You shall renew the face of the earth. Oh, Holy Spirit, grant us all the gifts to perfect the virtues, so we may live the beatitudes with Jesus Christ for the glory of the Father and the salvation of souls.

O Holy Spirit, substantial Love of the Father and the Son, uncreated Love dwelling in the souls of the just, come down upon me like a new Pentecost and bring me an abundance of Your gifts, of Your fruits, and of Your grace; unite Yourself to me as the most sweet Spouse of my soul. I consecrate myself entirely to You; invade me, take me, possess me wholly. Be the penetrating light which illumines my intellect, the gentle motion which attracts and directs my will, the supernatural energy which gives energy to my body.

Complete in me Your work of sanctification and love. Make me pure, transparent, simple, true, free, peaceful, gentle, calm, serene even in suffering, and burning with charity toward God and neighbor. Kindle in me the fire of Your love and the flame of eternal charity. Amen.

We read the following passage from Saint Paul's letter to the Ephesians for all of us, our families and the whole world:

For this reason, I kneel before the Father, from whom every family in heaven and on earth derives its name. I pray that out of his glorious riches he may strengthen you with power through his Spirit in your inner being, so that Christ may dwell in your hearts through faith.

And I pray that you, being rooted and established in love, may have power, together with all the Lord's holy people, to grasp how wide and long and high and deep is the love of Christ, and to know this love that surpasses knowledge—that you may be filled to the measure of all the fullness of God.

Now to him who is able to do immeasurably more than all we ask or imagine, according to his power that is at work within us, to him be glory in the church and in Christ Jesus throughout all generations, for ever and ever! Amen. (Eph 3:14-21)

- **1. The cenacle leader designates the people who will read the texts during the meeting.**
- **2. Reading of an extract from the Spiritual Diary of Elizabeth Kindelmann.**
- **3. Sharing of 15 to 20 minutes between the participants of the cenacle.**
- **4. Mention the prayer intentions.**

Flame of Love Opening Prayers for Cenacle

I confess to almighty God and to you, my brothers and sisters, that I have greatly sinned, in my thoughts and in my words, in what I have done and in what I have failed to do, through my fault, through my fault, through my most grievous fault; therefore, I ask blessed Mary ever-Virgin, all the Angels and Saints, and you, my brothers and sisters, to pray for me to the Lord our God."

"Let us take holy water and make the sign of the Cross five times, in honor of the five Holy Wounds of the Crucifixion of Our Lord Jesus Christ and recognizing that we are sinners:"

- **Meditate on offering ourselves to the Heavenly Father through the Wounds of Jesus. Here are three examples:**

Prayer (1)

✝ **Loving Jesus, in honor of the wound of your left hand.**
In the Name of the Father, and of the Son and of the Holy Spirit.

✝ **Loving Jesus, in honor of the wound of your right hand.**
In the Name of the Father, and of the Son and of the Holy Spirit.

✝ **Loving Jesus, in honor of the wound of your left foot.**
In the Name of the Father, and of the Son and of the Holy Spirit.

✝ **Loving Jesus, in honor of the wound of your right foot.**
In the Name of the Father, and of the Son and of the Holy Spirit.

✝ **Loving Jesus, in honor of the wound on your sacred side.**
In the Name of the Father, and of the Son and of the Holy Spirit. Amen.

Prayer (2)

✝ **Loving Jesus, deign to place in my soul the fruits of the wound of your left hand.**
In the Name of the Father, and of the Son and of the Holy Spirit.

✝ **Loving Jesus, deign to place in my soul the fruits of the wound of your right hand.**
In the Name of the Father, and of the Son and of the Holy Spirit.

✝ **Loving Jesus, deign to place in my soul the fruits of the wound of your left foot.**
In the Name of the Father, and of the Son and of the Holy Spirit.

✝ **Loving Jesus, deign to place in my soul the fruits of the wound of your right foot.**
In the Name of the Father, and of the Son and of the Holy Spirit.

✝ **Loving Jesus, deign to place in my soul the fruits of the wound on your side.**
In the Name of the Father, and of the Son and of the Holy Spirit.
Amen.

Prayer (3)

We offer ourselves to the Heavenly Father through all the wounds of our Savior, Jesus Christ.

✝ **We kiss the wound of your Sacred Left Hand, with sorrow deep and true,**
In the Name of the Father, and of the Son and of the Holy Spirit.

✝ **We kiss the wound of your Sacred Right Hand, with sorrow deep and true,**
In the Name of the Father, and of the Son and of the Holy Spirit.

✝ **We kiss the wound of your Sacred Left Foot, with sorrow deep and true,**
In the Name of the Father, and of the Son and of the Holy Spirit.

✝ **We kiss the wound of your Sacred Right Foot, with sorrow deep and true,**
In the Name of the Father, and of the Son and of the Holy Spirit.

✝ **We kiss the wound of your Sacred Side, with sorrow deep and true,**
In the Name of the Father, and of the Son and of the Holy Spirit.
Amen.

✝ Choose one of the three following prayers

PRAYERS TO SAINT MICHAEL THE ARCHANGEL

(1) SAINT MICHAEL THE ARCHANGEL, defend us in battle. Be our protection against the wickedness and snares of the devil. May God rebuke him, we humbly pray; and do Thou, O Prince of the heavenly host, by the power of God, cast into hell, Satan and all the evil spirits, who prowl about the world seeking the ruin of souls. Amen.

(2) O GLORIOUS PRINCE SAINT MICHAEL, chief and commander of the heavenly hosts, guardian of souls, vanquisher of rebel spirits, servant in the house of the Divine King and our admirable conductor, you who shine with excellence and superhuman virtue deliver us from all evil, who turn to you with confidence and enable us by your gracious protection to serve God more and more faithfully every day. Amen.

(3) THE 1890 PRAYER TO SAINT MICHAEL

- By Pope Leo XIII

"O glorious Archangel Saint Michael, Prince of the heavenly host, defend us in battle, and in the struggle which is ours "against the principalities and powers, against the rulers of this world of darkness, against spirits of evil in high places." (Eph 6:12)

Come to the aid of men, whom God created immortal, "made in his own image and likeness" (Wis 2:23), and redeemed "at a great price" (1 Cor 6:20) from the tyranny of the devil.

Fight this day the battle of the Lord, together with the holy angels, as already thou hast fought the leader of the proud angels, Lucifer, and his apostate host, "who were powerless to resist thee, nor was there a place for them any longer in Heaven. But that cruel, that

ancient serpent, who is called the devil or Satan, who seduces the whole world, was cast into the abyss with all his angels."
(Ap 12: 8-9)

Behold, this primeval enemy "and slayer of man" (Jn 8:44) has taken courage, "transformed into an angel of light" (2 Cor 11:14), he wanders about with all the multitude of wicked spirits, invading the earth in order to blot out the name of God and of His Christ, to seize upon, slay and cast into eternal perdition souls destined for the crown of eternal glory.

This wicked dragon pours out, as a most impure flood, the venom of his malice on men of depraved mind and corrupt heart, the spirit of lying, of impiety, of blasphemy, and the pestilent breath of impurity, and of every vice and iniquity.

These most crafty enemies have filled and inebriated with gall and bitterness the Church, the spouse of the Immaculate Lamb, and have laid impious hands on her most sacred possessions. In the Holy Place itself, where has been set up the See of the most blessed Peter and the Chair of Truth for the light of the world, they have raised the throne of their abominable impiety, with the iniquitous design that when the Pastor has been struck, the sheep may be scattered.

Arise then, O invincible Prince, bring help against the attacks of the lost spirits to the people of God, and bring them the victory.

The Church venerates thee as protector and patron; in thee holy Church glories as her defense against the malicious powers of this world and of hell; to thee has God entrusted the souls of men to be established in heavenly beatitude.

Oh! Pray to the God of peace that He may put Satan under our feet, so far conquered that he may no longer be able to hold men in captivity and harm the Church.

Offer our prayers in the sight of the Most High, so that "they may quickly conciliate the mercies of the Lord" (Ps 78:8), and beating down the dragon, the ancient serpent, who is the devil and Satan, do thou again make him "captive in the abyss, that he may no longer seduce the nations." (Ap 20:3) Amen.

Petition requested by the Virgin Mary

October 1962. A later note.

Elizabeth – "I am going to record what the Blessed Virgin told me in this year - 1962. I kept it inside for a long time without daring to write it down. It is a petition of the Blessed Virgin."

Virgin Mary – **"When you say the prayer that honors me, the Hail Mary, include this petition in the following manner:**

'Hail Mary, full of grace... Pray for us sinners, spread the effect of grace of thy Flame of Love over all of humanity, now and at the hour of our death. Amen."

Note: The competent bishop asked Elizabeth:

"Why the very old Hail Mary should be recited differently?"

On February 2, 1982, the Lord answered:

Jesus – **"It is exclusively thanks to the efficacious pleas of the Most Holy Virgin that the Most Holy Trinity granted the effusion of the Flame of Love. By it, ask in the prayer with which you greet My Most Holy Mother:**

'Spread the effect of grace of thy Flame of Love over all of humanity, now and at the hour of our death. Amen.'

So that, by its effect, humanity is converted."

Elizabeth –The Most Holy Virgin added:

Virgin Mary – **"I do not want to change the prayer by which you honor me; by this petition, I want rather to shake humanity. This is not a new prayer formula; it must be a constant supplication."**

Footnote: Let us pray the usual Rosary adding this supplication to each Hail Mary.

THE APOSTLES' CREED

I believe in God, the Father almighty,
Creator of heaven and earth,
and in Jesus Christ, his only Son, our Lord,
who was conceived by the Holy Spirit,
born of the Virgin Mary,
suffered under Pontius Pilate,
was crucified, died and was buried;
he descended into hell;
on the third day he rose again from the dead;
he ascended into heaven,
and is seated at the right hand of God the Father almighty;
from there he will come to judge the living and the dead.

I believe in the Holy Spirit,
the holy catholic Church,
the communion of saints,
the forgiveness of sins,
the resurrection of the body,
and life everlasting. Amen.

THE LORD'S PRAYER

Our Father, Who art in heaven, hallowed be Thy name; Thy kingdom come; Thy will be done on earth as it is in heaven.

Give us this day our daily bread, and forgive us our trespasses as we forgive those who trespass against us; and lead us not into temptation, but deliver us from evil.

THE FLAME OF LOVE "HAIL MARY"

Hail Mary, full of grace, the Lord is with Thee, blessed are Thou among women, and blessed is the fruit of Thy womb, Jesus.

Holy Mary, Mother of God, pray for us sinners, **SPREAD THE EFFECT OF GRACE OF THY FLAME OF LOVE OVER ALL OF HUMANITY,** now and at the hour of our death. Amen.

GLORY BE PRAYER

Glory be to the Father, and to the Son and to the Holy Spirit. As it was in the beginning, is now and ever shall be, world without end. Amen.

✝ Recite after each decade of the Rosary:

✝ O MY JESUS!

Forgive us our sins, save us from the fires of hell and lead all souls to Heaven, especially those in most need of Thy Mercy.

✝ COME HOLY SPIRIT!

Come by means of the power of the Flame of Love of the Immaculate Heart of Mary.

✝ MY ADORED JESUS! (UNITY PRAYER)

May our feet journey together;
May our hands gather in unity;
May our hearts beat in unison;
May our souls be in harmony;
May our thoughts be as one;
May our ears listen to the silence together;
May our glances profoundly penetrate each other;
May our lips pray together to gain mercy from the Eternal Father. Amen. (May 4,1962)

✝ Choose three invocations to Saint Joseph:

Saint Joseph, **Guardian of the Pure in Heart**, pray for us.
Saint Joseph, **Terror of Demons**, pray for us.
Saint Joseph, **Patron Saint of the Dying**, pray for us.
Saint Joseph, **Mainstay of Families**, pray for us.
Saint Joseph, **our Solace in Suffering**, pray for us.
Saint Joseph, **Protector of the Church**, pray for us.
Saint Joseph, **Hope of the Sick**, pray for us.
Saint Joseph, **Model of Labourers**, pray for us.

- **Sing a hymn to the Virgin Mary: "Ave Maria...".**
- **Repeat for each decade of the Rosary.**

The Meditated Rosary of the Flame of Love of the Immaculate Heart of Mary

Joyful Mysteries

Monday and Saturday

1 – The Annunciation

Grant us, Mary, by the graces of this mystery, a listening heart that responds to the call of the Lord with a loving yes joined to yours.

Virgin Mary – **"My little Carmelite, so many sins are committed in this country. Help me. Let us save the country. I place a beam of light in your hands; it is the Flame of Love of my heart. Add your love to this Flame and pass it on to others, my little one."** (Spiritual diary – April 13, 1962)

2 – The Visitation

Open our hearts, Mary, to give joyfully and without counting and in a gratuitousness of love, as you did at the Visitation.

Virgin Mary – **"I would like to place in your hands a new instrument, which I want you to accept and appreciate the importance of, because my heart looks upon my country with great affliction."**
(Spiritual diary – April 13, 1962)

3 – The Birth of Jesus

Mary, tenderness of the poor, make us discover the true wealth of the Kingdom, You who lived it at the birth of Jesus.

Virgin Mary – **"Take this Flame, my daughter, you are the first one I am handing it to. It is the Flame of Love of my heart. Ignite your own heart with it and then pass it on to others."**

Elizabeth – "The Blessed Virgin was sobbing so much that I could barely hear what she was saying. I asked her what I had to do. On behalf of the entire country, I promised her everything, so I could relieve her pain because my own heart was on the verge of shattering." (Spiritual diary – April 13, 1962)

4 – THE PRESENTATION OF JESUS IN THE TEMPLE

Grant us, Mary, that we may recognize the Light of God in our lives, as Simeon recognized it at the Presentation of Jesus.

Virgin Mary – **"My little one, I extend the effect of grace of the Flame of Love of my heart over all the peoples and nations, not only over those living in the Holy Mother Church, but over all the souls marked with the sign of the blessed Cross of my Divine Son." (...) "Also over those who are not baptized."** (Spiritual diary – September 16,1963)

5 – JESUS IS FOUND IN THE TEMPLE

Mary, who has welcomed in faith the mystery of the mission of your Son in the Temple, make us obedient to God's plan.

Virgin Mary – **"I can no longer hold back my Flame of Love in my heart. Let it leap out into all of you. (...)." "Those (the souls) accepting the Flame of Love will be intoxicated by the abundance of graces and they will proclaim everywhere, as I said before, that such a torrent of grace has never been granted since the Word became Flesh."** (Spiritual diary – November 7, 1963)

Luminous Mysteries

Thursday

1 – The Baptism in the Jordan

O Mary, who kept everything in your Heart, make us attentive to God's presence and grateful for the privileged grace of our baptism.

Jesus – **"Take courage. Look at Me. Always look into My eyes because in this new battle that Satan wants to wage against you, the look of My eyes will blind him. This will not happen quickly because I allow you to be tempted. May our glances profoundly penetrate each other."**
(Spiritual diary – January 14, 1963)

2 – The Wedding at Cana

O Mary, Virgin of Cana, ask Jesus to change our hearts so that we may live ever more in the great freedom of God's children.

Virgin Mary – **"Live in accordance with my graces so that Satan will be blinded even more and in an increasingly large range of action."**
(Spiritual diary – November 30, 1962)

3 – The Proclamation of the Kingdom

By your unceasing prayer, Mary, bring us to be authentic witnesses of the Good News of Jesus Christ.

Virgin Mary – **"You can only explain my Flame of Love to others by speaking about it. You have no right to be silent because of cowardice, pride, negligence or fear of sacrifice. Let the words you say about me be alive so the mystery of Heaven has an impact on souls."**
(Spiritual diary – July 26, 1971)

4 – The Transfiguration of Jesus

May our lives be transformed by the Holy Spirit, and may Your Flame of Love, Mary, guide our hearts as children.

Virgin Mary – **"Sacrifice and prayer! These are your instruments. The goal is to bring about the powerful work of Salvation. Oh, if your desires reach the throne of the heavenly Father, the results will be abundant."**
(Spiritual diary – July 22-23 1963)

5 – The Institution of the Holy Eucharist

O Mary, Virgin of Contemplation, help us to increase our intimacy with Jesus in the Eucharist, the Bread of Life of each day.

Virgin Mary – **(...) "The participation in the Holy Mass is what helps the most to blind Satan. Tormented and breathing out terrible vengeance, he wages a ferocious battle for souls since he feels the impending coming of his blindness."**
(Spiritual diary – November 22, 1962)

Sorrowful Mysteries

Tuesday and Friday

1 – The Agony in the Garden

"My Father, if it is possible, let this cup pass Me by, nevertheless, let it be as you, not I, would have it." With you, Mary, may this also become our prayer in our trials.

Jesus – **"My table is always set. I, the Host, have sacrificed everything. I give Myself."** (Spiritual diary – January 16, 1964)

2 – The Scourging at the Pillar

May our suffering, united to the scourging of Jesus, become a prayer offered with you Mary, for our family and for the world.

Jesus – **(...) "After receiving My Precious Blood, examine your souls and become aware of the exhilaration that the power of My Precious Blood brings about in you. Do not be so insensitive. Let not routine lead you to my holy table, but rather the fervor of sacrificial charity, which ignites through contact with My love. Through Me – inasmuch as you remain united to Me – it will burn sin out of your souls."** (Spiritual diary – January 16, 1964)

3 – The Crowning with Thorns

May the thorns which wound our heart make the garden of our life blossom in faith with You, Mary.

Jesus – **"With all the love of your heart, immerse yourself in My sorrowful Passion. When you arise in the morning, recall what was awaiting Me the entire day after the terrible torments of that night. (...) Contemplate the Way of the Cross and consider that I did not have any moment of rest."** (Spiritual diary – April 10, 1962)

4 – JESUS CARRIES THE CROSS

May our daily cross be made lighter by the sorrowful Cross of Jesus, which has become glorious by His Resurrection.

Jesus – **"During your daily tasks, you do not even think of Me within your souls. This hurts Me and I suffer so much. When you say: 'Lord, I am not worthy that You enter my house...'do not turn your back on Me, make yourselves worthy and dispose your hearts for constant union with Me."** (Spiritual diary – April 17, 1962)

5 – THE CRUCIFIXION

May the loving words uttered by Jesus on the Cross become seeds of life, love and forgiveness in every heart.

Jesus – **"From noon until 3:00 p.m., adore My Sacred Wounds. Hopefully you can keep fasting until the time My Sacred Body was taken down from the Cross."** (Spiritual diary – April 10, 1962)

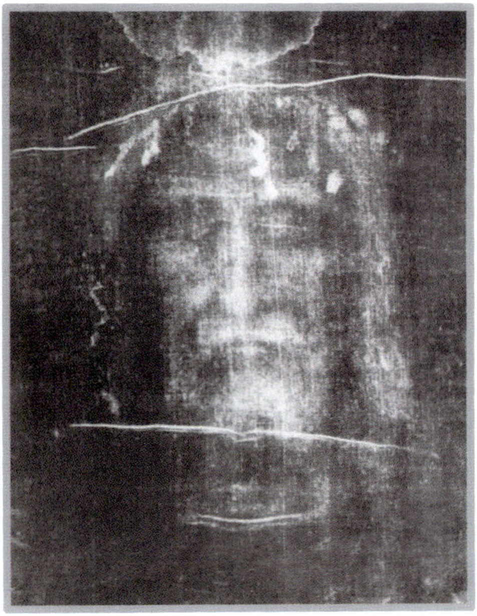

Glorious Mysteries

Wednesday and Sunday

1 – The Resurrection of Jesus

Through the power of Your Resurrection, grant us Lord the joy of life, and reach out to those who have lost its meaning.

Virgin Mary – **"When those persons consecrated to God and the faithful keep the Monday fast, they will free a multitude of souls from Purgatory each time they receive Communion during that week, at the very moment they receive the Holy Body of Our Lord Jesus Christ."** (August 15, 1980)

2 – The Ascension of Our Lord

"Why are you standing here looking into the sky? Go out and proclaim the Good News." May we become, O Lord, authentic witnesses of Your Resurrection.

Jesus – **"The Church and the whole world is in grave danger. Even with your strength, you cannot change this situation. The Most Holy Trinity alone can help you, through the concerted intercession of the Most Blessed Virgin, all the angels, all the saints, and those souls whom you have freed from Purgatory."** (Spiritual diary – August 15, 1980)

3 – The Descent of the Holy Spirit

Send forth Your Spirit, Lord, and give us the boldness of Your true disciples.

Elizabeth – "Jesus spoke to me at length about the time of grace and the Spirit of Love quite comparable to the first Pentecost, flooding the earth with its power. That will be the great miracle drawing the attention of all humanity. All that is the effusion of the effect of grace of the Blessed Virgin's Flame of Love." (Spiritual diary – March 24, 1963)

4 – THE ASSUMPTION OF MARY INTO HEAVEN

"I am the Resurrection and the Life." May these words, Mary, maintain us in the hope and the certainty of an eternal tomorrow.

Jesus – **"Trust in My Mother! She wipes away all doubt and removes fear by her boundless, motherly love. She marks you with a sign and will protect those who trust her. If you trust her, the depraved will be humiliated and thrown into the depth of hell. The future world is in preparation: The smile of My Mother will light up the whole earth.** (Spiritual diary – July 26, 1971)

5 – MARY'S CORONATION IN HEAVEN

O Mary, crowned in glory, enflame us continually by the Flame of Love of Your Immaculate Heart.

Virgin Mary – **"I grant to all the grace to see the results of their labors on behalf of my Flame of Love in each soul, in your country and in the entire world. You, who are laboring and making sacrifices for the prompt outpouring of my Flame of Love, you are going to get to see it."** (Spiritual diary – July 11, 1975)

✚ **After the last decade, pray the "Hail, Holy Queen":**

HAIL, HOLY QUEEN (Salve Regina)

HAIL, HOLY QUEEN, Mother of Mercy, our life, our sweetness, and our hope.

To thee do we cry, poor banished children of Eve. To thee do we send up our sighs mourning and weeping in this valley of tears.

Turn then, most gracious advocate, thine eyes of mercy toward us, and after this our exile show us the blessed fruit of thy womb, Jesus. O clement, O loving, O sweet Virgin Mary.

V. Pray for us, O Holy Mother of God.
R. That we may be made worthy of the promises of Christ.

Let us pray.

O God, whose only begotten Son, by His life, death, and resurrection, has purchased for us the rewards of eternal life, grant, we beseech Thee, that by meditating on these mysteries of the most holy Rosary of the Blessed Virgin Mary, we may imitate what they contain and obtain what they promise, through the same Christ our Lord. Amen.

Most Sacred Heart of Jesus, have mercy on us.

Immaculate Heart of Mary, pray for us.

✝ Say a prayer of your choice to Saint Joseph

(1) O GOD, who by your ineffable Providence has deigned to choose Saint Joseph as the husband of your Most Holy Mother, grant us, we ask you, that we may have for an intercessor in Heaven the one we venerate as protector on earth. Amen.

(2) O SAINT JOSEPH, you sought refuge for the Blessed Virgin in Bethlehem, help us to seek refuge for her Flame of Love in the hearts of all people. Amen.

(3) O SAINT JOSEPH, whose protection is so great, so strong, so prompt before the throne of God, I place in you all my interests and desires.

O SAINT JOSEPH, do assist me by your powerful intercession, and obtain for me from your Divine Son all spiritual blessings, through Jesus Christ, our Lord, so that, having engaged here below your heavenly power, I may offer my thanksgiving and homage to the most loving of fathers.

O SAINT JOSEPH, I never weary contemplating you and Jesus asleep in your arms; I dare not approach while He reposes near your heart. Press Him in my name and kiss his fine head for me and ask him to return the Kiss when I draw my dying breath. Saint Joseph, Patron of departing souls, pray for me. Amen.

(4) SAINT JOSEPH, TERROR OF DEMONS

Courageous Joseph, advised by an angel, you confront your fears of the unknown. Your light shines brightly, penetrating the dark corners of your being.

Your fears dispersed, you rediscover your true face, and actively participate in the divine project reuniting Mother and Child, and the people with their God. Together with Mary and Jesus, you dwell in the heart of God.

Help us to rediscover the united core of our identities, beyond all internal fears. Counsel us so we may build a better world to welcome the coming Kingdom.

Shed your light on our inner lives that, freed from the grip of our fears, our decisions may be founded in Love.
May the Face of God shine on us! Amen.

(5) SAINT JOSEPH, PATRON SAINT OF THE DYING

Faithful Joseph, with the fulfillment of the Lord's promise, you peacefully leave this world in Jesus' and Mary's arms.

Your faith transforms death into the sowing of life; thus, God considers you to be a just man.

Your heart overflows in the presence of the Lord. With your hands outstretched to God, your night is filled with prayers.

Surrounded by the living, you embark upon the great march to the promise Land.

Open our eyes that we may glimpse the road to Life that lies beyond death.

May nothing, not denial, anger, nor depression, separate us from the Love of God.

Strengthen our faith in God who always finds ways of preserving us in his friendship.

Be beside us to hold our hands when we take our first steps toward the Eternal Kingdom. Amen.

(6) SAINT JOSEPH, MAINSTAY OF FAMILIES

Attentive Joseph, in Mary and you, the Divine Word finds a favourable environment in which to carry out the will of the Father; thus, you become the family of the Child-God.

In your gentle life together, you experience Love daily. The unity of your hearts transforms life's lessons into growing wisdom and grace.

Open our hearts to the Word that lives within us, that our actions may bear witness to our connection to the family of God.
Sustain us in our emotional commitments, where giving and forgiveness shape our identities.
Grant us your tenderness in the things we do each day! Amen.

(7) SAINT JOSEPH, OUR SOLACE IN SUFFERING

Compassionate Joseph, one with us in our human condition, together with Mary and Jesus you experience exile, hunger and violence. Refusing vengeance, you choose mercy.

Your forgiveness breaks the circle of violence. Through your goodness, God's hope for our humanity is preserved. Joy is yours, for the Kingdom of God is your inheritance.

Open our compassionate hands in times of war, famine and exile. Keep us from developing a victim's mentality, and make our pain a source of growth.

Sustain us in fulfilling our responsibility of cultivating inner peace, joy and serenity.

In your wisdom, counsel us to close all doors to bitterness, so that, watched over by God, we may dance for joy. Amen.

(8) SAINT JOSEPH, PROTECTOR OF THE UNIVERSAL CHURCH

Brave Joseph, collaborator in God's project for humanity, your tenderness enfolds the newborn Church.

Saint Joseph's Oratory of Mount Royal

Just as Mary and Jesus recognize in you the protection of the Father, so too does the community of faith place itself under your protection.

Strengthen us with the Spirit that filled the Nazareth home and guide our footsteps on the road to the Kingdom.

Accompany us in carrying out our mission.

Help us to be lights in the world so that the family of God may spring forth from humanity transfigured in Christ.

Grant us the strength to imitate God's preference for the poor and weak. Guide us in our pastoral activities that our actions may be modeled on the Good News. Amen.

(9) SAINT JOSEPH, HOPE OF THE SICK

Benevolent Joseph, the Son of God placed his life in your hands. With Mary, you cared for Him who is the force of life.

May your compassion enfold our fragility, bringing us the comfort of the divine presence.

We join with you in prayer, saying:

"Lord Jesus, Son of the Living God, say a word for our healing!"

Make us sensitive to the illnesses of those close to us.

Support our efforts and grant us courage in the fight against all evil.

Help us to find meaning in God's great project for humanity beyond the sicknesses and sufferings that blind our sight.

The love of God be with us, as our hope lies with Him. Amen.

(10) SAINT JOSEPH, MODEL OF LABOURERS

Good Saint Joseph, when God wanted a family for his Son, He looked among the labourers, and chose you along with Mary, demonstrating His esteem for human work.

You put your heart into your work, and shared your workshop with Jesus. Your work, like that of other humans, found new meaning in the presence of God.

Sustain us in the hope of finding work when we are confronted with the desolation of unemployment.

Counsel business leaders to create an equitable division of labour that is respectful of individuals, and promotes our growth and happiness. Help us to perform our work joyfully, conscientiously, fairly and honestly. Prepare our hearts to recognize your Son in our colleagues at work. Amen.

(11) JOSEPH, GUARDIAN OF THE PURE IN HEART

Gentle Joseph, God is captivated by the quality of your heart. Your entire being is focused on doing his will. With Mary and Jesus, you answer the Holy Spirit's call to build a better world.

With one heart, we join you in saying:

"Here we are, Lord, Your will be done! Your Kingdom come nearer to us!"

Keep the hope of a new world alive in our hearts. Inspire us to speak words of tenderness to awaken the love of hearts.

May we draw the energy for our actions from the source of all Love so our faces may shine with the freedom of the children of God. Amen.

(12) TO YOU, O BLESSED JOSEPH,

Do we come in our tribulation and having implored the help of your most holy Spouse; we confidently invoke your patronage also.

Through that charity which bound you to the Immaculate Virgin Mother of God and through the paternal love with which you embraced the Child Jesus, we humbly beg you graciously to regard the inheritance which Jesus Christ has purchased by his Blood, and with your power and strength to aid us in our necessities.

O most watchful guardian of the Holy Family, defend the chosen children of Jesus Christ; O most loving father, ward off from us every contagion of error and corrupting influence; O our most mighty protector, be kind to us and from heaven assist us in our struggle with the power of darkness.

As once you rescued the Child Jesus from deadly peril, so now protect God's Holy Church from the snares of the enemy and from all adversity; shield, too, each one of us by your constant protection, so that, supported by your example and your aid, we may be able to live piously, to die in holiness, and to obtain eternal happiness in heaven. Amen. (By Pope Leo XIII)

✝ Conclude with the following two prayers:

PRAYER FOR THE HOLY FATHER'S INTENTIONS

Pray one *Our Father*, one *Hail Mary* and one *Glory Be* for the intentions of the Holy Father.

CONCLUDING PRAYER OF THE CENACLE

Eternal God, in whom mercy is endless and the treasury of compassion inexhaustible, look kindly upon us and increase Your mercy in us, that in difficult moments we might not despair nor become despondent, but with great confidence submit ourselves to Your holy will, which is Love and Mercy itself. (St. Faustina)

✝ Finally, make the Sign of the Cross five times in honor of each of the five Sacred Wounds of Our Lord Jesus Christ. (p.5)

✝ **The recitation of this Rosary is optional.**

The Chaplet of the Adored Jesus

The purpose of the chaplet is to help us grow from "saying" prayers with our lips to praying them from the heart and to help us move our spirituality from seeking salvation for ourselves to being deeply in love with God. Indeed, the key phrase of the chaplet is: "My adored Jesus, I love you." As simple as that is, saying it out loud can have a profound impact on our relationship with our Beloved.

It is also a powerful weapon against the rise of overt Satanism we see in many countries in the world. Our priests in the Philippines firmly believe that each profession of love for our Lord does as much to blind and weaken Satan as the Unity Prayer.

1. Petitions with Hail Mary

2. Meditation on the fives wounds

3. Creed, Our Father, Flame of Love Hail Mary (3) and Glory be

4. Large beads – The Unity Prayer. Small beads – "My Adored Jesus, I love you."

5. Chaplet conclusion: The Unity Prayer, Glory be, "My Adored Jesus, I love you" (3), a great Amen and Meditation on the five wounds.

The chaplet should be prayed after the Rosary and never in place of the Rosary or as a brief prayer in our Night Vigils. For consistency's sake and to follow Jesus' statement in the Diary, I suggest we use "My Adored Jesus" rather than "My Adorable Jesus" as the preface to the Unity Prayer when praying this Chaplet.

As a reminder, "My Adorable Jesus" as a preface to the Unity Prayer is not actually part of the prayer as given in the Diary. We include it to clarify to whom the prayer is addressed.

Peace and great Joy!

John A. Sullivan III
Director of Communication and International Dissemination
Flame of Love Movement

+ **The following prayers are optional.**

My Adored Jesus!

We ask the Lord Jesus to bring us in Spirit before His Eucharistic Presence throughout the world to adore Him. (Pause for silent reflection)

Prayer for the Dying

O most Merciful Jesus, Lover of souls, I pray Thee, by the agony of Thy Most Sacred Heart, and by the sorrows of Thy Immaculate Mother, cleanse in Thine Own Blood the sinners of the whole world who are now in their agony and to die this day. Amen.

Precious Blood prayer

"Dear Jesus moved by an impulse of love, and with purity of intention, I wish to cover my humble labors with Your merits and bathe them in the supernatural gold of Your Precious Blood.

I desire to consecrate my life to the saving of souls and the extension of Your glory, and I beg the Heavenly Father for as many souls as You shed drops of Blood during Your Passion."

(Sr. Josefa Menendez)

Memorare

Remember, O most gracious Virgin Mary, that never was it known that anyone who fled to thy protection, implored thy help, or sought thy intercession was left unaided.

Inspired with this confidence, we fly unto thee, O Virgin of virgins my Mother; to thee do we come; before thee we stand, sinful and sorrowful;

O Mother of the Word Incarnate, despise not our petitions, but in thy mercy hear and answer us. Amen.
(St. Louis-Marie Grignion de Montfort)

Apostolate Prayer

I desire to be a praying, living host, to bring Jesus to those I voyage with, to send out rays like a host.

Thank you, Jesus, for the souls you give me simply because I'm sure you give them to me.

I unite myself with the miracles you work in me.

I love you today more than yesterday, and tomorrow I shall love you more than today, because I have opened myself up to your grace, which is a torrent that ceaselessly engulfs me and continually transforms me into yourself and spreads out to others.

I pray for your mercy for all souls, for your mercy is limitless.

You died to save all souls; may not one sheep be lost!

I pray not only for the conversion of souls but for the perfection of souls.

Jesus, make us grow, bring us ever closer to you that we may all be united with you as a single flame.

May our hearts be channels of your torrents of graces, may we receive them to share them.

The Mass is the prayer of prayers, the prayer of Jesus.

I offer you, Lord, all the Masses, all my Communions, as well as this prayer. Amen.

Consecration of The Flame of Love Apostolate to the Immaculate Heart of Mary

Our Lady of Mount Carmel, Queen of Heaven and earth, and our Mother, through whom Almighty God has delighted to extend the most powerful outpouring of graces to mankind since the Word became flesh, we consecrate to your Immaculate Heart, completely and forever, the Flame of Love apostolate, formed to assist you in saving your children, accelerating your Triumph, and welcoming the Second Pentecost of the Holy Spirit, by spreading the effect of grace of your Flame.

We ask you to guide us in this, your apostolate, so that our planning conforms to your wishes and our efforts are always performed in your name, the Holy Name of Mary.

Enable us to grow, under your guidance so that the effect of grace of the Flame of Love will spread over all of humanity.

Send additional priests, and the faithful, who will embrace your endeavors, and help our apostolate to expand throughout this entire country and beyond.

Cover us with your Scapular of protection and your mantle of unity, harmony, and love; keep us steeped in humility so we do not falter. Strengthen us against the attacks of the enemy. Grant us the desire to share in the Redemptive activity of Your divine son.

Keep us strong, active and resolute; grant that our inevitable frustrations and failures will make us more determined than ever to continue our efforts, increasing your glory and thereby, the glory of Jesus, our Savior. We ask nothing in return but the pleasure of serving you.

Strengthen us in prayer and contemplation so that our apostolic actions may conform to your will and exceed expectations.

Most blessed Trinity, please approve our consecration and through Mary, our Mother, enable our apostolate to return lost sheep to your merciful bosom for all eternity. Amen.

Consecration
to the Immaculate Heart of Mary

(1)

O Immaculate Heart of Mary, ever-filled with kindness, show us Your Love. May the Flame of Love of Your Heart descend upon all men. We love You with all that we are. Instill true love in our hearts, that we may have toward You an unceasing devotion.

O Mary, who art meek and humble of Heart, remember us when we are in a state of sin. By means of Your motherly and Immaculate Heart, heal us from all our spiritual ailments and deficiencies.

Grant that we may always see the kindness of Your motherly Heart, and be converted by Your Flame of Love. Amen.

(2)

O Mary, the Father sent His Spirit to overshadow & empower you; His Son as your child to depend on you. I too give my whole self to you.

I consecrate myself to you, **O Mother and Queen**, my body with all its senses, my soul with all its faculties, my heart with all its affections, for you to give to Jesus and mold to His likeness.

Take all that I am, all that I have, and all that I do and give these to the Holy Spirit to form Jesus in me. At the foot of the Cross, He entrusted me to you; take and unite me to Jesus Crucified, humbly obedient to the Father, fully yielded to the Spirit in Love. May He be the Lord of my life and of men, and in His spirit, the praise and glory of the Father. Amen.

PRAYER FOR THE SPREAD OF THE FLAME OF LOVE

With the personal approval of His Holiness Paul VI
November 1973

BLESSED VIRGIN MARY OUR MOTHER,

Your love of God and Your love for us your children is such that You offer us to Your Divine Son Jesus on the Cross, to obtain forgiveness for our sins from the Eternal Father, and thus, obtain our salvation, and for anyone believing in Jesus not to perish but obtain Eternal Life.

It is with filial trust that we beseech you, Blessed Mother, with the Flame of Love of Your Immaculate Heart and through the Holy Spirit, to inflame in our hearts the fire of a perfect love for God and all men.

Help us to spread this Holy Flame to all people of goodwill, so that the Flame of Love may extinguish the fires of hate all over the world, and Jesus, the Prince of Peace, may be King, front and center, in every heart, in the Sacrament of His Love on the throne of our Altars. Amen.

Consecration to the Sacred Heart of Jesus

Act of consecration, revealed by Jesus to Saint Margaret-Mary Alacoque (1647-1690) during an apparition at Paray-Le-Monial.

I [ ] give myself and consecrate to the Sacred Heart of our Lord Jesus Christ, my person and my life, my actions, pains and sufferings, so that I may be unwilling to make use of any part of my being other than to honor, love and glorify the Sacred Heart. This is my unchanging purpose, namely, to be all His, and to do all things for the love of Him, at the same time renouncing with all my heart whatever is displeasing to Him. I therefore take You, O Sacred heart, to be the only object of my love, the guardian of my life, my assurance of salvation, the remedy of my weakness and inconstancy, the atonement for all the faults of my life and my sure refuge at the hour of death.

Be then, O Heart of goodness, my justification before God the Father, and turn away from me the strokes of his righteous anger. O Heart of love, I put all my confidence in You, for I fear everything from my own wickedness and frailty, but I hope for all things from Your goodness and bounty.

Remove from me all that can displease You or resist Your holy will; let your pure love imprint Your image so deeply upon my heart, that I shall never be able to forget You or to be separated from You.

May I obtain from all Your loving kindness the grace of having my name written in Your Heart, for in You I desire to place all my happiness and glory, living and dying in bondage to You.

Amen.

EXCERPT FROM THE CONSECRATION TO THE IMMACULATE HEART OF MARY

By St. John Paul II – Fatima, May 13, 1982

(Prayer of Deliverance)

O IMMACULATE HEART OF MARY!

Help us to conquer the menace of evil, which so easily takes root in the hearts of the people of today, and whose immeasurable effects already weigh down upon our modern world and seem to block the paths towards the future!

From famine and war, deliver us.

From nuclear war, from incalculable self-destruction, from every kind of war, deliver us.

From sins against the life of man from its very beginning, deliver us.

From hatred and from the demeaning of the dignity of the children of God, deliver us. From every kind of injustice in the life of society, both national and international, deliver us.

From readiness to trample on the commandments of God, deliver us.

From attempts to stifle in human hearts the very truth of God, deliver us.

From the loss of awareness of good and evil, deliver us.

From sins against the Holy Spirit, deliver us, deliver us.

Accept, O Mother of Christ, this cry laden with the sufferings of all individual human beings, laden with the sufferings of whole societies.

Help us with the power of the Holy Spirit to conquer all sin: individual sin and the "sin of the world," sin in all its manifestations.

Let there be revealed, once more, in the history of the world the infinite saving power of the Redemption: the power of merciful Love!

May it put a stop to evil! May it transform consciences!

May your Immaculate Heart reveal for all the light of Hope!

Amen.

Prayer for the Beatification of Elizabeth Kindelmann

Dear God, you granted Elizabeth the gift of ardent love toward you. This made her worthy to be the one through whom the world may know the Flame of Love of the Immaculate Heart of the Blessed Mother. The source of her zeal was Christ present in the Blessed Sacrament, whom she accepted in her heart and adored with devotion every day.

Filled with the Bread of eternal life, she gave an example through prayer, fasting, sacrifice, penance and reparation for sanctification and for saving souls.

Grant us, Lord that we may follow her in practicing virtues, and if it accords with your intention, we may honor her on our altars soon. Our Blessed Mother, spread the effect of grace of your Flame of Love over all of humanity, now and at the hour of our death. Amen.

Testimonies of prayers answered through Elizabeth's intercession are to be sent to the Flame of Love Movement:

Szeretetláng Mozgalom;
1029 Budapest
Álmos vezér u. 22, Hungary
e-mail: szeretetlang.hu@gmail.com

LITANY OF THE SACRED HEART

Lord, **have mercy on us.**
Christ, **have mercy on us.**
Lord, **have mercy on us.**
Christ, **hear us.**
Christ, **graciously hear us.**

God the Father of Heaven, **Have mercy on us.**
God the Son, Redeemer of the world, **Have mercy on us.**
God the Holy Spirit, **Have mercy on us.**
Holy Trinity, one God, **Have mercy on us.**

Heart of Jesus, Son of the Eternal Father**, Have mercy on us.**
Heart of Jesus, Formed by the Holy Ghost in the womb of the Virgin Mother, **Have mercy on us.**
Heart of Jesus, Substantially united to the Word of God, **Have mercy on us.**

Heart of Jesus — **Have mercy on us.**

Of Infinite Majesty, (repeat after each line)
Holy Temple of God,
Tabernacle of the Most High,
House of God and Gate of Heaven,
Burning Furnace of charity,
Vessel of Justice and love,
Full of goodness and love,
Abyss of all virtues,
Most worthy of all praises,
King and center of all hearts,
In Whom are all the treasures of wisdom and knowledge,
In Whom dwelleth all the fulness of the Divinity,
in Whom the Father is well pleased,
Of Whose fullness we have all received,

Heart of Jesus — **Have mercy on us.**

Patient and abounding in mercy,
Rich unto all who call upon Thee,
Fountain of life and holiness,
Atonement for our sins,
Filled with reproaches,
Bruised for our offenses,
Made obedient unto death,
Pierced with a lance,
Source of all consolation,
Our Life and Resurrection,
Our Peace and Reconciliation,
Victim for our sins,
Salvation of those who hope in Thee,
Delight of all the Saints, **Have mercy on us.**

. Lamb of God Who takest away the sins of the world, **Spare us, O Lord.**

. Lamb of God Who takest away the sins of the world,

Graciously hear us, O Lord.

. Lamb of God Who takest away the sins of the world, **Have mercy on us.**

R. **Jesus, meek and humble of heart,** V. **Make our hearts like unto Thine.**

Let us pray.

Almighty and eternal God, look upon the Heart of Thine most-beloved Son, and upon the praises and satisfaction He offers Thee in the name of sinners; and appeased by worthy homage, pardon those who implore Thy mercy, in Thy Great Goodness in the name of the same Jesus Christ Thy Son, Who liveth and reigneth with Thee, in the unity of the Holy Ghost, world without end. Amen.

Litany Of The Blessed Virgin Mary
[The Litany of Loreto]

Lord, **have mercy.**
Christ, **have mercy.**
Lord, **have mercy.**
Christ, **hear us.**

Christ, **graciously hear us.**
God, the Father of Heaven,
have mercy on us.
God the Son, Redeemer of the World,
have mercy on us.
God the Holy Spirit, **have mercy on us.**
Holy Trinity, One God, **have mercy on us.**

Holy Mary, pray for us.
Holy Mother of God, (repeat after each line)
Holy Virgin of Virgins,
Mother of Christ,
Mother of the Church,
Mother of Mercy,
Mother of Divine Grace,
Mother of Hope,
Mother most Pure,
Mother most Chaste,
Mother Inviolate, **Pray for us.**
Mother Undefiled,
Mother most Amiable,

Mother most Admirable,
Mother of good Counsel,
Mother of our Creator,
Mother of our Savior,
Virgin most Prudent,
Virgin most Venerable,
Virgin most Renowned,
Virgin most Powerful,
Virgin most Merciful,
Virgin most Faithful,
Mirror of Justice,
Seat of Wisdom,
Cause of our Joy,
Spiritual Vessel,
Vessel of Honor,
Singular Vessel of Devotion,
Mystical Rose,
Tower of David,
Tower of Ivory,
House of God,
Ark of the covenant,
Gate of heaven,
Morning star, **Pray for us**
Health of the sick,
Refuge of sinners,
Solace of Migrants,
Comfort of the afflicted,
Help of Christians,

Queen of Angels,
Queen of Patriarchs,
Queen of Prophets,
Queen of Apostles,
Queen of Martyrs,
Queen of Confessors,
Queen of Virgins,
Queen of all Saints,
Queen conceived without original sin,
Queen assumed into Heaven,
Queen of the most Holy Rosary,
Queen of the Family,
Queen of Peace,

Lamb of God, Who take away the sins of the world, **spare us, O Lord.**
Lamb of God, Who take away the sins of the world, **graciously hear us, O Lord.**
Lamb of God, Who take away the sins of the world, **have mercy on us.**

V. **Pray for us, O Holy Mother of God.**
R. **That we may be made worthy of the promises of Christ.**

Let us pray

Grant, we beg Thee, O Lord God, that we Thy servants, may enjoy lasting health of mind and body, and by the glorious intercession of the Blessed Mary, ever Virgin, be delivered from present sorrow and enter into the joy of eternal happiness. Through Christ our Lord. **Amen.**

LITANY OF ST JOSEPH

Lord, have mercy. **Lord, have mercy**.
Christ, have mercy. **Christ, have mercy.**
Lord, have mercy. **Lord, have mercy.**
Jesus, hear us. **Jesus, graciously hear us.**

God, the Father of Heaven. **Have mercy on us.**
God, the Son, Redeemer of the world. **Have mercy on us.**
God, the Holy Spirit. **Have mercy on us.**
Holy Trinity, One God. **Have mercy on us.**

Holy Mary. **Pray for us.** (Repeat after each line)

St. Joseph.
Renowned offspring of David.

Light of Patriarchs,
Spouse of the Mother of God,
Chaste guardian of the Virgin,
Foster father of the Son of God,
Diligent protector of Christ,
Head of the Holy Family,
Joseph most just,
Joseph most chaste,
Joseph most prudent,
Joseph most strong, **Pray for us.**
Joseph most obedient,
Joseph most faithful,
Mirror of patience,
Lover of poverty,
Model of artisans,
Glory of home life,
Guardian of virgins,
Pillar of families,
Solace of the wretched,
Hope of the sick,
Patron of the dying,
Terror of demons,
Protector of Holy Church, **Pray for us.**

. Lamb of God, who take away the sins of the world. **Spare us, O Lord**.
Lamb of God, who take away the sins of the world. **Graciously hear us, O Lord.**
. Lamb of God, who take away the sins of the world**. have mercy on us**.

V. **He made him the lord of his household.**
R. **And prince over all his possessions.**

Let us pray

O God, in your ineffable providence you were pleased to choose Blessed Joseph to be the spouse of your most holy Mother; grant, we beg you, that we may be worthy to have him for our intercessor in heaven whom on earth we venerate as our Protector: You who live and reign forever and ever. Amen.
Saint Joseph, pray for us . The Lord's Prayer.

LITANY OF THE SAINTS

The Litany of the Saints reminds us of a moving line about them from one of the Eucharistic prayers to God the Father said at Mass: "May their merits and prayers gain us Your constant help and protection."

Keep in mind that God also calls on us to be saints. If this seems like too tall an order, remember that, with God's help we can live our lives reflecting His love and goodness, letting Him work through us, just like He's done with the saints! May this litany, and others like it, help us all to be "citizens-in-training" for heaven!

Lord, **have mercy on us.**; *Christ,* **have mercy on us.** ;
Lord, **have mercy on us**.
Christ, **hear us**; *Christ,* ***graciously hear us.***

God the Father of heaven, ***have mercy on us.*** (repeat after each line)
God the Son, Redeemer of the world,
God the Holy Ghost,

Holy Trinity, one God,
Holy Mary, ***pray for us*** (repeat after each line)
Holy Mother of God,
Holy Virgin of virgins,

St. Michael,
St. Gabriel,
St. Raphael,
All you holy angels and archangels,
All you holy orders of blessed spirits,
St. John the Baptist,
St. Joseph,
All you holy patriarchs and prophets,
St. Peter,
St. Paul,
St. Andrew,
St. James,

Pray for us

St. John,
St. Thomas,
St. James,
St. Philip,
St. Bartholomew,
St. Matthew, **Pray for us**
St. Simon,
St. Thaddeus,
St. Matthias,
St. Barnabas,
St. Luke,
St. Mark,
All you holy apostles and evangelists,
All you holy disciples of our Lord,
All you holy innocents,
St. Stephen,
St. Lawrence,
St. Vincent,
SS. Fabian and Sebastian,
SS. John and Paul,
SS. Cosmas and Damian, **Pray for us**
SS. Gervase and Protase,
All you holy Martyrs,
St. Sylvester,
St. Gregory,
St. Ambrose,
St. Augustine,
St. Jerome,
St. Martin,
St. Nicholas,
All you holy bishops and confessors,
All you holy doctors,
St. Anthony,
St. Benedict,
St. Bernard,
St. Dominic,
St. Francis, **Pray for us**
All you holy priests and levites,
All you holy monks and hermits,
St. Mary Magdalen,
St. Agatha,
St. Lucy,
St. Agnes,
St. Cecilia,
St. Catherine,
St. Anastasia,
All you holy virgins and widows,
All you holy men and women, saints of God, ***intercede for us.***
Be merciful, ***spare us, O Lord. intercede for us.***
Be merciful, ***graciously hear us, O Lord. intercede for us.***
From all evil, ***deliver us, O Lord***. (repeat after each line)
From all sin, ***deliver us, O Lord***.

From Thy wrath, ***deliver us, O Lord***
From a sudden and unprovided death,
From the deceits of the devil,
From anger, and hatred, and all ill-will,
From the spirit of fornication,
From lightning and tempest,
From the scourge of earthquakes,
From plague, famine and war,
From everlasting death,
By the mystery of Thy Holy Incarnation,
By Thy Coming,
By Thy Nativity,
By Thy Baptism and Holy Fasting,
By Thy Cross and Passion,
By Thy Death and burial,
By Thy holy Resurrection,
By Thine admirable Ascension,
By the coming of the Holy Ghost, the Paraclete.
On the day of judgment.

Deliver us, O Lord

We sinners, *we beseech Thee,* ***hear us*** (repeat after each line)
That Thou wouldst spare us,
That Thou wouldst pardon us,
That Thou wouldst bring us to true penance,
That Thou wouldst vouchsafe to govern and preserve Thy Holy Church,
That Thou wouldst vouchsafe to preserve our Apostolic Prelate, and all ecclesiastical orders in holy religion,
That Thou wouldst vouchsafe to humble the enemies of holy Church,
That Thou wouldst vouchsafe to give peace and true concord to Christian kings and princes,
That Thou wouldst vouchsafe to grant peace and unity to all Christian peoples,
That Thou wouldst vouchsafe to bring back to the unity of the Church all who have strayed away, and lead to the light of the Gospel all unbelievers,
That Thou wouldst vouchsafe to confirm and preserve us in Thy holy service,
That Thou wouldst lift up our minds to heavenly desires,
That Thou wouldst render eternal blessings to all our benefactors,
That Thou wouldst deliver our souls, and the souls of our brethren, relatives, and benefactors from eternal damnation,
That Thou wouldst vouchsafe to give and preserve the fruits of the earth,
That Thou wouldst vouchsafe to grant eternal rest to all the faithful departed,
That Thou wouldst vouchsafe graciously to hear us, Son of God.

Hear us.

Lamb of God, who takest away the sins of the world, ***spare us, O Lord.***
Lamb of God, who takest away the sins of the world, ***graciously hear us, O Lord.***
Lamb of God, who takest away the sins of the world, ***have mercy on us.***
Christ, **hear us**.
Christ, ***graciously hear us.***
Lord, **have mercy on us**.
Christ, ***have mercy on us.***
Lord, **have mercy on us.**

The Lord's Prayer

April 10,1962

Elizabeth – One day, He said:

Jesus – **"My daughter, I'm now going to specify how each day of the week should be allocated. If you remember, I began to speak about this previously. However, I put this off until today to include more things in your schedule.**

Come, if you have time. If you have plenty of it, tell Me. The decision is yours. I respect your free will completely. You flatter Me if you abandon it spontaneously to Me."

✞ MONDAY: THE DAY OF THE HOLY SOULS

Jesus – **"Let all your actions be done with the purpose of helping them.**

In union with Me, desire that these souls contemplate My Face as early as possible. Offer for them the strict fast as well as prayers during a part of the night.

I do not ask this strict fast and prayer just from you. Make public these requests jointly with other messages from My Heart:

Anyone fasting on bread and water on Monday will free each time the soul of a priest from the place of suffering. (*)

Whoever practices this will receive the grace of being liberated from the place of suffering within eight days after their death.

Our Mother herself is asking for this. Her appeal to her Flame of Love obliges Me to fulfill her request."

(*) Editor's Note: Purgatory

This supposes that the person has died in the grace of God. In a private conversation, **Elizabeth said:** "In different places in the Diary it speaks of freeing the souls. Each time I would have had to write **'If they had died in the grace of God.'** This fact appeared so evident to me that it seemed superfluous."

✞ TUESDAY: OFFER THIS DAY FOR THE FAMILY

Jesus – **"Make spiritual communions for each member of the family. Offer each person, one by one, to our dear Mother. She**

will take them under her protection. You will also offer that evening vigil for them."

Elizabeth – "Lord, I usually sleep deeply. What if I cannot wake up to keep watch?"

Jesus – **"I will help you with that as well. If there's anything too difficult for you, confidently tell our Mother. She also spent many nights in prayer vigils. My daughter, you must be responsible for your family leading them to Me, each in his own particular way. Ask for My graces on their behalf unceasingly. We will work together and I cannot do without your support. Your most worthy patron is Saint Joseph. Do not forget him, invoke him every day. He will gladly help making our Cause a success."**

✞ WEDNESDAY: A DAY FOR PRIESTLY VOCATIONS

Jesus – **"Ask Me for many young men with a fervent heart. You will get as many as requested because the desire lies in the soul of many young men but there is no one helping them to realize their goal. Do not be overwhelmed. Through the prayers of the night vigil, you can obtain abundant graces for them."**

✞ THURSDAY: REPARATION TO THE BLESSED SACRAMENT

Jesus – **"On that day, you will spend hours in My sacred Presence. Adore Me with great fervor making reparation for the many offenses inflicted upon Me. Offer the strict fast for the twelve priestly souls."**

(This request was specifically for Elizabeth, but if you want to fast, it will certainly be appreciated by Jesus)

"Offer also the nocturnal vigil for them. Immerse yourself into My sorrowful agony as I was sweating blood. You will draw great spiritual strength from it."

✞ FRIDAY: THE DAY OF MY PASSION

Jesus – **"With all the love of your heart, immerse yourself in My sorrowful Passion. When you arise in the morning, recall what was awaiting Me the entire day after the terrible torments of that night.**

While at work, contemplate the Way of the Cross and consider that I did not have any moment of rest. Totally exhausted, I was forced to climb the mount of Calvary. There is much to contemplate. I went to the limit, and I tell you, you cannot go to excess in doing something for Me.

From noon until 3:00 p.m., adore My sacred Wounds. Hopefully you can keep fasting until the time My sacred Body was taken down from the Cross. Then, on that day, offer the night prayer for the twelve priests. If you accept to sacrifice yourself, My daughter, you will receive an even greater abundance of graces."

✝ SATURDAY: THE DAY OF OUR MOTHER

Jesus – **"On this day, venerate our Mother in a special way with a very particular tenderness.**

As you are well aware, she is the Mother of all graces. Wish that she be venerated on earth as she is venerated in Heaven by the multitude of angels and saints. Seek for agonizing priests the grace of a holy death. Offer every moment of the day for that purpose. What a great reward you will receive! In Heaven, priestly souls will intercede for you and the Most Holy Virgin will be waiting for your soul at the hour of your death. Offer the night vigil for this intention also."

✝ SUNDAY

Elizabeth – For this day, the loveable Redeemer gives no specific directions.

(This conversation took place approximately in July, but no specific date.)

Virgin Mary – **"Even on Sunday, your day of rest, you will do vigils and attend as many Masses as possible. Offer them for the youth. Think of the many children guided every year to my Divine Son. How many souls are lost, not taking root because no one is concerned about their spiritual progress. Offer these days especially for the young. Even when my Most Holy Son was tired, He wanted the children to come to Him. That is why you also must never be tired. You know it is Him who asked you to continually share in His work of Redemption."**

EXPLANATION ON FASTING

Jesus gives us a very affectionate invitation to make sacrifices for souls. He knows how many souls are lost, and that's why He intervenes with this grace of the Flame of Love, which surpasses all those He granted after His Resurrection. The Virgin Mary has also been urging us for years in her various apparitions. In a time determined by God, we have reached the point of Satan's blindness. Whether we like it or not, it is indeed the blinding of Satan by the Flame of Love, and this great grace is given to us for this precise reason. In this way, souls will be able to decide without hindrance to choose to follow Jesus and enter eternity with Him.

A number of people have asked us: "What should I do with the fasting Jesus asks of me?"

We'll try to explain it here.

It's easy for someone in good physical condition to fast strictly on bread and water without damaging their health. Not so for those with physical difficulties or who are taking medication for certain illnesses.

What was asked of Elizabeth Kindelmann is not necessarily asked of everyone. A person can give what they can, not what they cannot. Jesus knows us, and we are not all challenged in the same way. Some people will undertake severe fasts, but that's between Jesus and the soul concerned, it's really a very personal thing.

In a journey with Jesus, we all start with the first day; so, one day at a time. If you read the Spiritual Diary, you'll see that Elizabeth had also experienced difficulties, and you'll see how Jesus even allowed her to eat at the evening meal because she wasn't in good physical condition.

Persevere With Me

April 10, 1962

Jesus – **"Do not worry, My dear little Carmelite. Do not think, 'How will I make the Cause prevail?' I work with chosen souls. Be satisfied with being good. Do you know how to be a good Carmelite? Live humbly. Live the hidden contemplative life in union with Me. Refrain your tongue and be on guard not to say unneeded words.**
My love for you knows no limits, My little Carmelite. Do you know how happy I am when you accept the sacrifices I offer you? (He said this with great tenderness.) **Persevere with Me! By this, you make Me happy. Desire many souls for Me so I can distribute My graces to them."**

Elizabeth – While I was prostrate before Him, He said:

Jesus – **"Do you know that I was awaiting you with a sad heart? You see how lonely I am! You are the only one here. If you did not come, I would be an orphan.**
You were an orphan, My little one, and you know how bitter it is."

Elizabeth – He kept talking and instructing me.

Jesus – **"I always tell you not to worry that you can give Me only little things. I say again, always remain little. Do you know what we are going to do? You will give Me the little pieces of a mosaic which you collect throughout the day. I will arrange these pieces according to their color and shape. When all is finished, you will marvel to see the work of art that I created. But I cannot be an artist unless you gather the pieces. Without you, I cannot bring about My work of art."**

Elizabeth – Jesus said all of this with a pleading voice.

May 2, 1962

Elizabeth – (…) since the Lord Jesus deprived me of both His words and His presence, a great dryness was consuming my soul. As I knelt speechless, I remembered the Lord's words:

Jesus – **"One Our Father or one Hail Mary prayed in the midst of spiritual dryness is much more fruitful than exuberant prayers of someone who abounds in spiritual favors."**

Community Prayer

Elizabeth – "As I recalled these words, I felt a great calm in my spiritual dryness. As I was kneeling there on this May afternoon, I heard the chanting of the Litany of the Blessed Virgin. I never experienced before the power to raise up my soul to such great fervor that came from this community prayer."

Announce My Mercy – Sacrifice Yourself

May 4, 1962

The Savior said:

Jesus – **"I choose you, My little one, to be the bearer of My divine mercy. Fill yourself with the abundance of My divine mercy and when you open your mouth to speak, proclaim the mercy of My Heart burning of desire for sinners.**
Let your whole life be a burning desire to take part in My work of Redemption through prayer, sacrifice and desire."

Elizabeth – "How many times, good Jesus, I have written down Your sad complaints, but I can do very little."

Jesus – **"Let your heart burn with desire, My little one. Just with that, you lessen the burning sorrow of My Heart. If all the souls consecrated to My Heart yearned just as I would, the number of those making reparation would increase. You know, they form a large group. If all took part with their heart and soul, by prayers and sacrifices, in My work of Redemption, I would not complain so much. Love Me more, My little one, and serve Me with greater surrender. Do not let the power of routine take control."**

May 1962

Jesus – **"Each morning, present to Me the offering of your sacrifices; place it at the door of My tabernacle, it will ignite at the fire of My love. During the day, let not the flame of your sacrifices fade away. See to it that the love of many victim souls rise up to Me, and through My intercession, obtain the mercy of the heavenly Father."**

Remain In My Work Of Redemption

October 4, 1962

Elizabeth – While I was praying the litanies with exposition of the Blessed Sacrament, the Lord Jesus surprised me with His words.

Jesus – **"Today you are very distracted and have hardly lifted your soul to Me. Why do you abandon Me? I long for your words and for each vibration of your soul."**

Elizabeth – "Pardon me, my beloved Jesus." As I was repentant and immersed in Him, the litanies began. When I lifted up my eyes towards the monstrance where He rested in His immaculate light, I looked at Him with deep homage. At that moment, it seemed like the monstrance moved and turned slightly toward me.

The Lord's unlimited love poured out into my heart. With my eyes closed, in deep humility and conscious of my misery, I offered myself to Him. I gave Him all my weakness because I had nothing else to offer Him.

Light For My Church

October 5, 1962 – First Friday

Jesus – **"Today, My Heart joyfully awaits all the souls. I will pour out upon all of you My extraordinary graces. Take advantage of this moment in which I distribute such richness.**

My daughter, be the window of the Church which My divine grace makes bright and shining. To make this a reality, you must continually work so that through you, the divine Sun can shine upon all those in My Holy Church who are close to your soul. Your window receives the brightness of My splendor and transmits its light. Those who are close to you will feel the divine Sun shining upon them through you. This will make the fruit of My work of Salvation more abundant in souls."

Elizabeth –. The Lord Jesus told me this after Holy Communion. At the same time, the Blessed Virgin began to speak with maternal goodness.

Virgin Mary – **"My little one, I unite you firmly with me. The Flame of my heart, that I entrusted you, will project onto you its rays of abundant graces. This will continue even in Heaven. With my maternal hand, I bless your drops of oil which you collect so zealously.**

With motherly love, I will await your arrival in Heaven. The drops of oil resulting from your sufferings will fall on the earth into the lamps that are either extinguished or barely flickering in the souls, and they will ignite at my Flame of Love. You, therefore, can take your place beside me until the end of the world."

The Graces Received By Mothers

October 9, 1962

Elizabeth – Today, while I was with the Savior, He infused the joy of His Heart into my soul.

Jesus – **"How wonderful that you have come. How I awaited you! At other times, I told you to be immersed in Me like a drop of water in wine. I am the wine, you are the water. Just be united with Me and you will be astonished. Only I will reign in you. My Body and Blood give strength and life to all of you. How happy you will be to receive more of My life-giving strength. Gather with Me."**

Elizabeth – With sadness, I complained to the Lord Jesus that the Evil One seeks to destroy the peace of our family. "Oh, give us peace!" I asked for abundant graces that My children live in God's grace. He allowed me to hear His consoling voice.

Jesus – **"When you are in Heaven and from up there you contemplate the death of one of your children, you will be by his bed. Your drop of oil will fall on the empty lamp and the Flame of Love of the Blessed Virgin will be lit. This great outpouring of graces will save souls from damnation. They will experience your motherly hand caressing them. Also, you will feel the great power which your many sufferings possess. These souls will also experience your hand which will help them at the moment of death. They will see your meritorious life on earth which they do not now appreciate."**

New Trials

December 1, 1962

Virgin Mary – **"My little one, I see your great anguish. You fear the long road and the new trials demanded of you by my Flame of Love. Be humble, valiant and decisive. I will accompany you. You possess the Spirit of Love; His strength accompanies you and enlightens the souls to whom you are sent."**

Elizabeth – The Blessed Virgin also showed me the disposition of those souls who will receive her Flame of Love. As she spoke, her words filled me with strength.

Virgin Mary – **"On this road, you must accept generously the many painful misunderstandings and humiliations. The one to whom I send you is also suffering. He is tormented by sorrow and doubt, even more than you are. My little one, you and those to whom I send you must suffer, pray and fast much, so that one way or another you can gain merits so as to reveal my Flame of Love that is proceeding with great hindrance. I deliberately send it to souls that struggle with doubts. I do this so they feel the effusion of the effect of grace of my Flame of Love. Then they will believe and trust in me."**

Salvation Of Souls

May 16, 1963

Elizabeth – While I was cooking, the Lord Jesus said:

Jesus – **"I beg you, in the future, do not think about yourself. May your thinking be only: us! If you come to Me and if you think of Me, think that the two of us are one. Let there be no gap between us. I will fill with grace the empty parts of your soul, and you, deny yourself so that, although you keep living, it will be I who live within you and you live only through Me."**

Elizabeth – Then He said again:

Jesus – **"How we love you, My little one!"**

Elizabeth – A few days later:

Jesus – **"And I tell you: From now on, no longer speak of yourself. The 'I' in you must cease completely. Let there be only Me for you. That is your real life."**

May 17, 1963

Elizabeth – In the morning, I knelt at the Communion rail, but when the priest saw that I was the only one to receive, he did not give me Holy Communion. I said, "Oh, how painful this was for us!"

Jesus – **"That is true. Let our joys and our pains be as one. Now, we both feel that we have been set aside and we are in pain. Let us endure this grief together."**

Elizabeth – Now, this is easier to accept. A deep feeling for Him overwhelmed my soul.

Jesus – **"You are My little drop of water. Immerse yourself in the intoxicating wine of My infinite Divinity, both in its life-giving power and in its sweet aroma that you pour out for Me. May My good aroma pour out around you. When others perceive it, they will be led to Me. You see, we must be one.**

Do not be bound by the clay of the earth filled with worms. Let the earth be only that for you. Look at it as such and let us save souls from the worms that threaten and swarm them. Do penance and pray for them. Your acceptance of the sacrifice is the salt that, once poured over the swarming worms, they will fall like dead leeches. Let them be shriveled and annihilated. Let us have just one thought: the salvation of souls."

Publications of the Flame of Love Movement in Canada

. Conference of Father Gabriel Róna
. Declaration of his Eminence Cardinal Péter ERDÓ

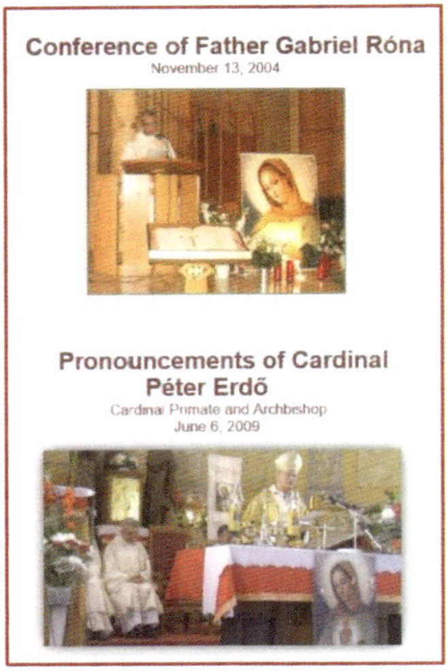

This conference was given by Father Gabriel Róna on November 13, 2004, in Montreal, during the 3rd national congress.

Father Gabriel makes an important link with the Fatima apparitions: the triumph of the Immaculate Heart of Mary announced at Fatima takes place through this great grace of the Flame of Love!

In the same document, we offer you the statement of His Eminence Cardinal Péter ERDŐ, Primate of Hungary and Archbishop of Esztergom-Budapest, regarding the Association "Movement Flame of Love of the Immaculate Heart of Mary".

This 22-page booklet is available in English and French.

History of the Flame of Love Movement

This booklet presents the history of the Flame of Love Movement from its beginnings with Elizabeth Kindelmann, in Hungary.

It is very useful to learn about the different countries where the Flame of Love Movement has spread.

The 36-page booklet is also available in French and Spanish.

The Souls in Purgatory

This 12-page booklet contains the messages of Jesus and Mary, who ask us to help the souls in Purgatory to enter heaven as soon as possible.
Available in English and French.

Blinding Satan with the Flame of Love Novena

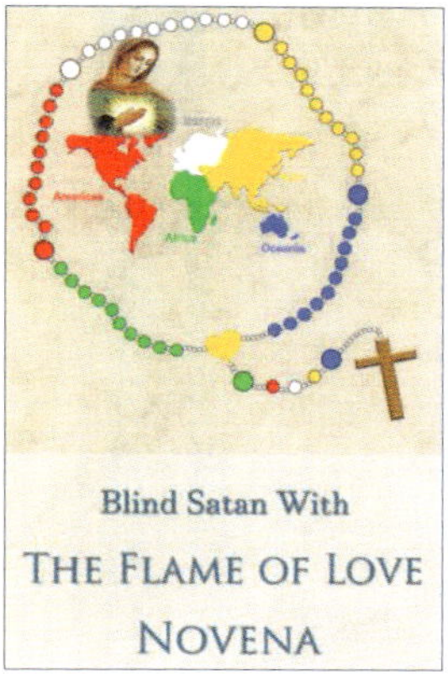

The Novena booklet has been much appreciated since we began to distribute it.

The Mysteries of the Rosary are at the end of this 40-page booklet.

Also available in French, English and Spanish (36p.).

The Unity Prayer Booklet

This 41-page the Unity Prayer booklet contains various messages from the Spiritual Diary of Elizabeth Kindelmann, in which Jesus often quotes excerpts from the Unity Prayer He revealed to her on May 4, 1962.

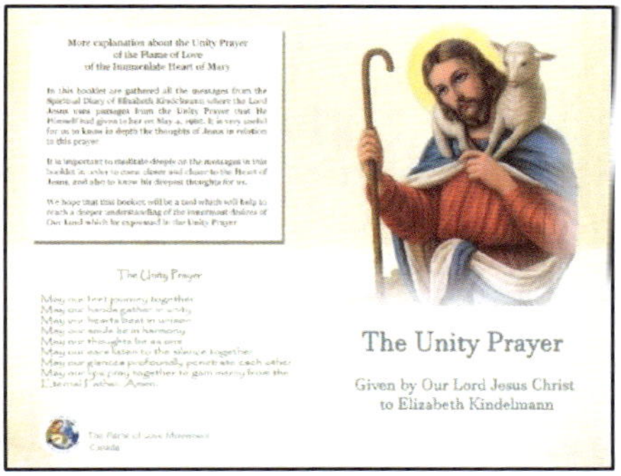

The main purpose of this booklet is to show the reader that this prayer—which is also very effective in blinding Satan—has a prominent place in the Spiritual Diary.

Available in English and in French.

PART I: LOVING WHILE BEING LOVED
PART II: LEARNING TO LOVE

From the Flame of Love Spiritual Diary

Fr Domonkos Mészáros, op

Assistant Director for the Flame of Love Movement in Hungary

Parts I & II – 75 pages

DEACON NORMAN ALEXANDER of the Diocese of Memphis in Tennessee has endeavored to write about the wonderful gift of the Flame of Love of the Immaculate Heart of Mary. Saved by the Flame of Love, follows Unity and the Flame of Love published February of 2019. He is committed to promoting the Flame of Love because there has never been a time of grace like this since the Word became flesh. These are the words of Jesus and Mary, and we know them to be trustworthy.

Unity and the
FLAME OF LOVE
2 Booklets
Part I & Part II
54 pages

Saved by the
FLAME OF LOVE
2 Booklets
Part I & Part II
63 pages

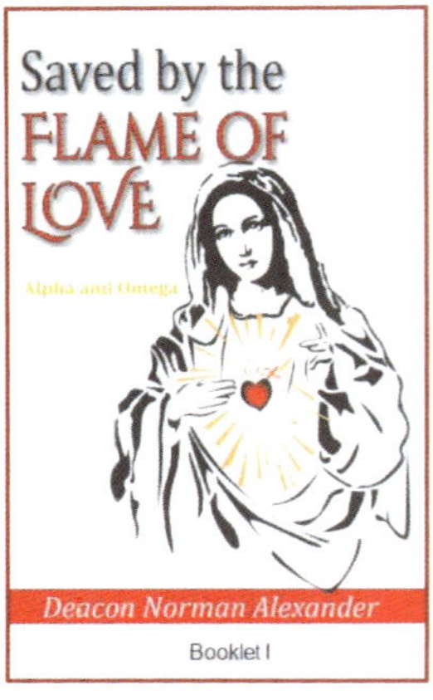

by

Deacon Norman Alexander